Devouring Flames

Devouring
Flames

The Story of Forest Fires

By Meredith Costain

NATIONAL GEOGRAPHIC

WASHINGTON D.C.

One of the world's largest nonprofit scientific and educational organizations, the National Geographic Society was founded in 1888 "for the increase and diffusion of geographic knowledge." Fulfilling this mission, the Society educates and inspires millions every day through its magazines, books, television programs, videos, maps and atlases, research grants, the National Geographic Bee, teacher workshops, and innovative classroom materials. The Society is supported through membership dues, charitable gifts, and income from the sale of its educational products. This support is vital to National Geographic's mission to increase global understanding and promote conservation of our planet through exploration, research, and education.

For more information, please call
1-800-NGS-LINE (647-5463) or write to the following address:
National Geographic Society
1145 17th Street N.W.
Washington, D.C. 20036-4688
U.S.A.

For information about special discounts for bulk purchases, please contact
National Geographic Books Special Sales at ngspecsales@ngs.org

Visit the Society's Web site: www.nationalgeographic.com

Copyright © 2006 National Geographic Society

Text revised from *Forest Fires* in the National Geographic Windows on Literacy program from National Geographic School Publishing, © 2004 National Geographic Society

All rights reserved. Reproduction of the whole or any part of the contents without written permission from the publisher is prohibited.

Published by National Geographic Society. Washington, D.C. 20036

Design by Project Design Company

Printed in the United States

Library of Congress Cataloging-in-Publication Data

Costain, Meredith.
Devouring flames : the story of forest fires / by Meredith Costain.
    p. cm. -- (National Geographic science chapters)
"Text revised from Forest Fires in the National Geographic Windows on Literacy program from National Geographic School Publishing."
Includes bibliographical references and index.
ISBN-13: 978-0-7922-5944-2 (library binding)
ISBN-10: 0-7922-5944-0 (library binding)
1. Forest fires--Juvenile literature. 2. Forest fires--Prevention and control--Juvenile literature. I. National Geographic Society (U.S.) II. Title. III. Series.
SD421.23.C67 2006
634.9'618--dc22

2006016318

Photo Credits
Front Cover: © Raymond Gehman/CORBIS; 2-3: © David R. Frazier/ Stone/ Getty Images; 6: © Carlo Allegri/ Getty Images; 7: © Peter Essick/ IPN Stock; 8: © Justin Sullivan/ Getty Images; 9: © Sally A. Morgan/ Corbis; 10: © David McNew/ Getty Images; 11: © Layne Kennedy/ Corbis; 12: © Howard M. Paul; 14-15: © Marc Solomon/ The Image Bank/ Getty Images; 16: © Bruce Chambers/ Corbis; 17: © Mike Blake/ Reuters; 18-19: © Mike Goulding/ Corbis; 19 (bottom): © Index Stock; 20-21: © Bill Stormont/ Corbis; 22-23: © Howard M. Paul; 24: © Marcio Jose Sanchez/ Associated Press; 26: © Dan Lamont/ Corbis; 27: © Roger Archibald/ Portfolio.com; 28: © Theo Allofs/ zefa/ Corbis; 29: © Australian Picture Library/ Corbis; 30 31: © Howard M. Paul; 32: © Corbis and The Smoky Bear Licensing Program. The Name and character of Smokey Bear are the property of the United Stated as provided by 16 U.S. C. 580 p-1 and 18 U.S.C. 711, and are used with the permission of the Forest Service, U.S. Department of Agriculture; 33: © NASA/ Science Photo Library; 34: © Cheryl Richter; 35: © Roy Morsch/ Corbis.

Contents

A firefighter knows how
to stay safe in a forest fire.

Into the Fire

The firefighter sees a red wall of flames. Ash and burning leaves land all around her. The smoke stings the firefighter's eyes. The heat makes her skin feel like it's burning. The firefighter is scared, but she knows what to do. She has been trained to keep herself and her team of firefighters safe.

Forest fires can quickly
burn out of control.

Chapter 1

How Do Forest Fires Start?

Forest fires can start when lightning hits dry grass or trees. However, lightning strikes aren't the only way that fires start. People acting carelessly cause most forest fires.

Sometimes hikers forget to put out campfires properly. They can drop cigarettes or matches on the ground. Trash can cause fires, too. An empty glass bottle can reflect the sun's rays. These rays can heat the dry grass so much that it bursts into flames.

Trash, such as glass bottles, can cause forest fires.

A forest fire burns dangerously close to houses.

Forest fires may burn out of control. They can kill many plants and animals that live in forests. Forest fires can spread to places where people live. This puts people, pets, houses, crops, and farm animals in danger.

Fire chiefs decide on a plan of attack for fighting a forest fire in California.

Fire Science

Fire needs three things to make it burn: oxygen, heat, and fuel. This is called the Fire Triangle. Each side of the triangle stands for one of these three things. Fires can be extinguished, or put out, if one side of the triangle is taken away.

A fire burns all the available fuel in a forest.

Oxygen   FIRE   Heat

Fuel

Oxygen is a gas in the air around us. A fire cannot burn without oxygen.

Fuel is what is burned in a fire. Fuel in a forest can be dead leaves, dry grass, twigs, and branches.

Heat starts the fire and keeps it burning. It also helps the fire spread. Heat might come from a match, a campfire, or lightning.

Fire Facts

- The fire season in the United States begins in the early spring and runs through October.
- Most large fires take place in the mountainous western states.
- The giant walls of flames in a forest fire can burn acres of land in just a few minutes.

A forest fire burns out of control in California.

- On average, nearly 4.2 million acres of land are destroyed by wildfires each year in the United States.
- The number of forest fires increases as more houses are built near forests.
- In 2004 there were nearly 80,000 forest fires in the U.S. These fires burned close to seven million acres. It cost nearly $900,000 to fight these fires.

A firefighter sprays
foam on a forest fire.

Chapter 2

Firefighters

The men and women of the Forest Service care for forests by preventing, controlling, and fighting forest fires. These firefighters risk their lives to protect people who may be caught near a fire. They also work to protect property near the fire and the forest itself. It takes a large team of hard-working firefighters to control a forest fire.

▶ Firefighters pump water onto a blaze in California.

Hand Crews

Some firefighters work in a group called
a hand crew. These firefighters battle the
flames with chain saws and shovels. They
fight fires by taking the fuel away from the
fire. Hand crews use their tools to make
firelines, or bare strips of earth. They do this
by chopping down shrubs and trees. They
also clear away grass and leaves.

A member of a hand crew uses a shovel to build a fireline.

◀ Firefighters clear brush to create a fireline.

The hand crew works quickly to stop the flames from spreading. They must be careful to stay safe. All hand crews have a safety zone they can move to if the fire gets too close. A safety zone is a place where the fire can't reach them.

A hand crew extinguishes hot spots left from a forest fire.

After the main fire has been put out, hand crews still have work to do. They check that there are no "hot spots" left burning. Hot spots are small areas of heat or fire. If hot spots are not put out completely, they can restart the fire.

Hotshot Crews

Imagine hiking three miles in less than an hour while wearing a heavy backpack. That's what the members of a hotshot crew have to do. Hotshot crews get their name from working near the hottest part of a fire.

Each hotshot crew has 20 members. They are trained to look out for each other.

Hotshot crews carry a lot of firefighting equipment.

Hotshot crews use pumps, axes, and chain saws to fight forest fires. They work to take the heat out of the fire by pumping water on it. They also remove fuel from the fire's path.

Hotshot crews often work very long shifts. Sometimes they have to sleep on the ground in safety zones. Hotshot crews also search for people in danger and rescue them.

A helicopter fights a
forest fire from the air.

Helicopters

Forest fires can be fought from the air. Helitacks are firefighting crews who slide down ropes from helicopters into the forest. After the fire has been put out, helitack teams hike out of the forest.

Firefighters also use helicopters to look for forest fires and to see how big a fire is. Helicopters can be used to drop large amounts of water onto fires. They can also deliver equipment to fire crews on the ground. Helicopters were first used to fight fires in 1947.

▶ A firefighter drops into the forest from a helicopter.

Smokejumpers

Smokejumpers are firefighters who jump out of a plane and parachute down to fight a forest fire. Forest fires can start many miles away from roads in rugged, mountainous areas. It might take hours, or even days, for firefighters to walk through the forest to the fire. This would give a small fire time to become a large fire.

Smokejumpers can parachute into forests and start fighting the fire almost as soon as it is discovered. Smokejumpers take everything they need with them. A smokejumper carries enough food and water to survive for two days before help arrives!

◀ A smokejumper stands on a runway with his equipment.

Smokejumpers fight
fires in areas that are
hard to reach.

The Forest Service alerts visitors to the fire danger during fire season.

FIRE DANGER

LOW

TODAY!

PREVENT WILDFIRES

Chapter 3

Preventing Forest Fires

Forest fires can spread very quickly. One way to prevent unwanted forest fires is to teach people fire safety. For example, hikers should always have a bucket of water and a shovel to put out their campfire.

Campers shovel dirt on a campfire to put it out.

The Forest Service has other ways to prevent fires. When members of fire crews are not fighting fires, they "thin" the forest. This means that they remove fallen or dead trees and branches that could be fuel for a forest fire.

A firefighter starts a controlled burn.

A Forest Service worker cuts down a dead tree.

Sometimes the Forest Service lights fires to prevent fires! This is called controlled burning. Firefighters light a small fire to burn some of the fuel in a forest. This type of fire is safe because the firefighters are ready to put the fire out. If a forest fire comes to a place that has had a controlled burn, it cannot become a big fire. There is too little fuel left to burn.

Smokey Bear

The Forest Service also prevents forest fires by increasing public awareness about fire safety. The cartoon character Smokey Bear has been a part of American life since 1944. He has been featured on posters and signs that remind people to be careful with cigarette butts, matches, and campfires.

LEASE!

SMOKEY

Only you can
PREVENT FOREST FIRES

YOURS TO ENJOY

NOT TO DESTROY

PLEASE! Only you can
PREVENT FOREST FIRES

SMOKEY

PLEASE FOLKS,
be *extra* careful
this year!

Remember- Only you can
PREVENT FOREST FIRES !

Smokey Bear has
been promoting fire
safety for more than
60 years.

Chapter 4

A New Forest Grows

Forest fires can also help a forest. Fire can clear away layers of dead leaves, logs, and needles from the forest floor. This makes room for new shrubs and trees to grow. Some kinds of trees need the heat from a fire in order to release their seeds. The new seeds can get plenty of water and sunlight in the burned forest.

New trees grow in a burned forest.

How to Write an A+ Report

1. Choose a topic.
- Find something that interests you.
- Make sure it is not too big or too small.

2. Find sources.
- Ask your librarian for help.
- Use many different sources: books, magazine articles, and websites.

3. Gather information.
- Take notes. Write down the big ideas and interesting details.
- Use your own words.

4. Organize information.
- Sort your notes into groups that make sense.

- Make an outline. Put your groups of notes in the order you want to write your report.

5. Write your report.

- Write an introduction that tells what the report is about.

- Use your outline and notes as you write to make sure you say everything you want to say in the order you want to say it.

- Write an ending that tells about your report.

- Write a title.

6. Revise and edit your report.

- Read your report to make sure it makes sense.

- Read it again to check spelling, punctuation, and grammar.

7. Hand in your report!

Glossary

controlled burning	clearing land of grass, leaves, and twigs by lighting small fires
extinguish	to put out a fire
fireline	a strip of cleared land that stops a fire from spreading
hand crew	firefighters who clear away the fuel of a fire
helitack	a firefighting crew that is taken to a forest fire by helicopter
hot spot	a small area of heat or fire that is still burning after the main fire has been put out
prevent	to stop something from happening
safety zone	a place where firefighters can move to if a fire gets too close
smokejumper	a firefighter who parachutes from a plane to fight forest fires

Further Reading

• Books •

Nonfiction

Platts, Linda. *Forest Fires (Criticial Thinking About Environmental Issues)*. San Diego, CA: Greenhaven Press, 2004. Ages 9-12, 112 pages.

Trumbauer, Lisa. *Forest Fires.* London: Franklin Watts, 2005. Ages 9-12, 64 pages.

Fiction

Duey, Kathleen, Karen A. Bale, and Bill Dodge. *SURVIVAL! Forest Fire, Minnesota, 1984.* New York, NY: Aladdin, 1999. Ages 9-12, 160 pages.

Ingold, Jeanette. *The Big Burn.* San Diego, CA: Harcourt Children's Books, 2002. Young adult, 304 pages.

• Websites •

All About Fires

National Geographic Society
http://www.nationalgeo
graphic.com/eye/wildfires/
wildintro.html

USDA Forest Service
http://www.fs.fed.us/fire/

Public Broadcasting Service
http://www.pbs.org/wgbh/
nova/fire/

National Interagency
Fire Center
http://www.nifc.gov/index.
html

Environmental Literacy
Council
http://www.enviroliteracy.org/
article.php/46.html

Wildfire Prevention

USDA Forest Service
http://www.smokeybear.com

Federal Emergency
Management Agency
(FEMA)
http://www.fema.gov/kids/
wldfire

Index